# D&O: What You Need to Know

by Melanie L. Herman
and Leslie T. White

Copyright © 1998
by the Nonprofit Risk Management Center

*All Rights Reserved.*

ISBN 0-9637120-8-X

**Nonprofit
Risk Management
Center**
1001 Connecticut Avenue, NW
Suite 410
Washington, DC 20036
(202) 785-3891
Fax: (202) 296-0349
http://www.nonprofitrisk.org

## About the Nonprofit Risk Management Center

The Nonprofit Risk Management Center is dedicated to helping community-serving nonprofits prevent harm, conserve resources, preserve assets, and free up resources for mission-critical activities. The Center provides technical assistance on risk management, liability, and insurance matters; publishes easy-to-use written materials; designs and delivers workshops and conferences; and offers competitively priced consulting services.

The Center is an independent nonprofit organization that does not sell insurance or endorse specific insurance providers. For more information on the products and services available from the Center, call (202) 785-3891 or visit our web site at http://www.nonprofitrisk.org.

## Acknowledgments

The authors are grateful to the following persons who provided thoughtful comments and suggestions on the draft of this publication:

Kimberly D. Coran, *Executive Risk*

Pamela Davis, *Nonprofits' Insurance Alliance of California*

Lou Novick, *The Novick Group, Inc.*

Tim Paul, *Westport Insurance Corporation*

David Szerlip, *David Szerlip & Associates*

*This publication is designed to provide accurate and authoritative information in regard to the subject matter covered. It is distributed with the understanding that the publisher is not engaged in rendering legal, accounting, or other professional service. If legal advice or other expert assistance is required, the services of a competent professional should be sought.* From a Declaration of Principles jointly adopted by a Committee of the American Bar Association and a Committee of Publishers.

# Table of Contents

# Introduction

The Children's Place, a day care facility for the children of low income families, was experiencing wonderful growth and success in recent years. The board of directors had recently decided to expand the nonprofit's services from caring for only three and four-year-olds to include infants and toddlers as well. The expansion in service meant that they would have to purchase the building they were currently leasing so that an addition could be built for a second playroom and a nursery.

When they offered to buy the building and the owner declined, the board of directors chose to move into a larger facility which could better accommodate the needs of The Children's Place, even though two years remained on their rental agreement. In the meantime, another tenant moved into the old building immediately.

Three years later, the owner's son files suit against The Children's Place for breach of contract and failure to pay rent. He claims that his mother (the owner) has not been able to make sound business decisions on her own for many years and that the board of directors of The Children's Place was aware of her condition at the time of their request to purchase the building. Currently, he is attempting to have his mother committed to a psychiatric facility while the legal wrangling is still going on. Both The Children's Place and the son have incurred substantial attorney and court fees with no decision in sight.

This could happen to any nonprofit. What would happen if this occurred to your organization? Does your nonprofit have sufficient resources (financial and personnel) to respond to the lawsuit and pay any subsequent settlement or judgment? Of course, since you have directors' and officers' liability insurance (D&O), your insurance company will handle it. Maybe. Your first response should be to submit the suit papers to your insurer. However, whether or not your organization has coverage and how the policy will respond depends upon the how the coverage is written. Unfortunately, you and your board cannot assume that your D&O policy will cover this loss and all of its expenses. Does your policy cover — past, present, and future directors and officers, the organization, allegations of fraud, defense costs? Every insurance company's D&O policy is different, providing different coverages, limitations, and exclusions. The purpose of this book is to help you better understand the coverages and limitations of D&O policies.

In 1991, the Nonprofit Risk Management Center published a pamphlet on directors' and officers' liability insurance titled *D&O—Yes or No?*. At that time, the booklet title captured a frequent question posed by nonprofits, "Should we purchase directors' and officers' liability coverage?" The D&O landscape — both in terms of today's nonprofit buyers and commercial or alternative market sellers — has changed dramatically since the early 1990s. In recognition of these considerable changes, we offer this new book that asks — and hopefully answers — some of the most important, pressing questions about liability coverage for nonprofits and nonprofit boards of directors.

To protect a nonprofit's core assets — its people, property, income, and goodwill — a range of strategies are necessary. Before purchasing insurance, nonprofit managers should take time to learn more about the organization's exposures, assess its available resources, minimize the risk of loss through prevention activities, and understand the insurance marketplace and the specific policies that are available. Without question, nonprofits today are becoming increasingly sophisticated businesses. Most nonprofit executives and boards recognize the need to apply sound business principles in the management of operations including the oversight of purchasing. Despite this fact, too many nonprofits fail to give the insurance buying process more than scant attention. Routinely, many renew outdated insurance policies that are also a poor match for the organization's exposures. Some nonprofits avoid the process of bidding their insurance program for a number of reasons such as a perceived lack of time and resources or the fear of disturbing a comfortable relationship with a local insurance agent. Others rely exclusively on the advice of professional advisors with potential conflicts of interest — such as the insurance agent serving on the board of directors. This publication is designed to help nonprofit managers and board members better understand one specific form of liability coverage: directors' and officers' liability insurance. Our specific goals in publishing this book are to:

- Educate readers about the role of insurance in a comprehensive risk management plan.

- Inform readers about the nature of D&O exposures and the types of events that might lead to claims covered under a typical D&O policy.

- Empower nonprofits to get the most out of every dollar allocated for insurance.

- Encourage every nonprofit board and CEO to devote the time needed to understand their D&O policy.

- Inspire readers to start at the beginning — consider their exposures and risk control options before examining D&O insurance as a financing tool.

- Encourage readers to develop more effective relationships with their professional advisors, including an insurance expert. This booklet is not a substitute for expert professional help. Every nonprofit needs a group of independent, competent advisors, including an insurance professional.

- Alert nonprofit managers to some weaknesses in D&O policies for nonprofits. An inadequate policy can be worse than no policy. It may provide a false sense of security and result in the failure to integrate other risk management measures.

For readers who do not have D&O coverage currently, this publication is an excellent starting point. It will help you determine if and why you need coverage, how to purchase coverage, and other measures necessary to minimize your D&O exposure. For those who purchase D&O coverage already (including those who have experienced a claim), this book will help you reevaluate the role of D&O insurance in your insurance and risk management program. This book will also help you review many of the key policy provisions. We hope that after reading this book you'll dust off your D&O policy and take a second look. Do not regard this booklet as a substitute for the advice of an attorney or professional insurance advisor. We strongly urge you to consult with qualified legal and insurance professionals before procuring liability coverage or making any changes in your current coverage.

In case you were looking... this book offers no easy answers to the questions, "Do we need D&O insurance?" and "How much coverage should we buy?" While reading this publication will require an hour or two of your time, we promise that it will pay dividends in the years to come. Instead of dreading the annual renewal process for your D&O policy, you may look forward to the opportunity to save your nonprofit some money or purchase greater protection by knowing exactly what to look for in a policy.

# Chapter 1
# About Risk Management

**R**isk management is *a discipline for dealing with uncertainty.* Risk management provides a framework and process for identifying, controlling (minimizing or avoiding), and financing risks. In the nonprofit sector, the most effective risk management activities are the ones that prevent injuries or property losses/damage in the first place. Without exception, preventing harm (to people and property) is less costly than paying for injuries and property damage.

While there are many lessons and ideas to learn from this publication, one of the most important themes is the role of insurance in a risk management program. Contrary to popular belief, risk management and insurance are not synonyms. A nonprofit does not manage risk simply by purchasing insurance. Nonprofits deal with *uncertainty* through careful planning and the use of common sense. The risk management process involves:

1. Acknowledging and identifying risks,

2. Evaluating and prioritizing risks,

3. Selecting and implementing strategies to control and finance risks, and

4. Monitoring and updating the program.

To look at it in a different way, managing risk in a nonprofit organization requires asking and answering three key questions:

1. **What can go wrong?** — What harm might come to our people, property, financial assets (including sources of revenue), and reputation?

2. **What will we do?** — both to prevent harm and in the aftermath of harm occurring despite our best efforts.

3. **How will we pay for it?** — Do we have sufficient resources on hand to pay for losses we anticipate? If a claim is filed, what funding sources might we tap for defense costs and a potential judgment or settlement?

As indicated above, you determine how to pay for or finance anticipated losses after you consider potential harm (what could go wrong?) and the strategies for preventing or minimizing the likelihood of harm (what will we do?).

For example:

■ When Elvira Gulch, the new executive director at the American DoGood Organization, took over the position last winter, she took an immediate dislike to Dorothy Gale, a loyal clerk who had been employed there for 14 years.

Dorothy was well liked by the board of directors and the volunteers. Gulch enjoyed no such popularity and decided to fire Dorothy. She did not document the reasons for her decision or consult DoGood's general counsel before taking action.

Elvira was surprised to learn that Dorothy filed a suit alleging wrongful termination and age discrimination. The court ruled in Dorothy's favor, and after many years as a clerk making only $390 per week, Dorothy was awarded a lump sum of $19,500.

■ Learning that employee terminations account for 60 percent of all nonprofit D&O claims, the board of directors at the Hillside Health Clinic decides to take measures to reduce this risk. The board consults with a local employment attorney to establish a termination policy. They include the new policy in the employee handbook and provide training to all supervisors on the proper procedures for terminating an employee. Senior managers monitor the implementation of the policy, ensuring that when supervisors recommend terminating an employee, they follow the proper steps. The termination procedures include submitting to Hillside's executive director and attorney for review a summary of the reasons for termination, the warnings given to the employee, and all written performance reviews. After a thorough review, the executive director can authorize the supervisor to dismiss the employee. Despite the procedures, a terminated employee can still allege "wrongful termination" and file a claim. The board decides to purchase D&O insurance to fund potential losses from allegations of wrongful employment practices.

Decisions about how to pay for losses focus on those risks that cannot be avoided. Employment-related risks cannot be eliminated unless your nonprofit operates without employees. Employment risks, like other risks such as someone getting hurt while participating in your program, can be controlled effectively so that claims are rare. However, your organization must be prepared to pay for those losses that do occur. Three risk financing options are available to nonprofits:

1.  *Retention* or the use of the organization's funds to pay for losses. The money can come from operating funds, fund balances and reserves, or borrowing money from a bank or other source;

2.  *Contractual transfer* which is when the nonprofit transfers the financial burden of a loss to another party through an indemnification agreement or a hold harmless agreement; and

3.  *Commercial insurance* through an insurance company or an alternate provider such as a charitable risk pool or risk retention group.

Insurance is a popular option among nonprofits. Insurance is not, however, a suitable financing strategy for every risk. Some risks are uninsurable by law or commercial practice such as liability coverage for criminal acts or in some states punitive damages. Many coverages are too expensive. For claims with high frequency but low severity (such as dog bites at an animal shelter), it may make sense to choose a deductible above the value of this type of regular loss. Most nonprofits, however, choose a low or no deductible to avoid unexpected expenses. However, it may be better for the organization to pay for all claims up to a predetermined level as a way to control insurance costs. Many larger organizations with substantial financial resources rely on insurance to fund only catastrophic losses.

# Chapter 2
# Managing Governance Risks

## A. Know Your Legal Duties

State laws governing the establishment and operation of corporations (including incorporated nonprofits) support a basic premise: the board of directors of a corporation is responsible for the affairs of the corporation. As such, individual board members may be held personally accountable for their actions.

The term "fiduciary duty" is often used to describe the responsibility owed by a board member. It refers to the capacity in which a director or officer renders services to the organization. A nonprofit board member is expected to act in good faith, using prudent judgment. Board members owe the legal duties of loyalty, obedience, and care to the nonprofit itself, its members, and under some circumstances, to third parties. The standards of conduct a nonprofit board must adhere to come from rules that have developed out of community customs ("common law") as well as federal and state statutes. Because it is based largely on public policy and is shaped by evolving norms and community standards, common law is a moving target. It is subject to ongoing and varying interpretation in the courts.

The personal liability of a nonprofit director for actions taken on behalf of the organization depends upon whether or not a duty to act in a certain manner existed. If no statutory standard exists, common law standards are examined. These standards are based on the following duties:

1.  The **duty of loyalty** requires that officers and directors act in good faith, avoid activities that will harm the organization, and not allow their personal interests to prevail over the interests of the organization.

The duty of loyalty requires that nonprofit board members avoid self-dealing — transactions with the nonprofit in which they are involved and interested, or using their positions of trust for personal advantage. Self-dealing goes beyond simple theft or embezzlement and includes the use of the organization's funds for personal benefit (such as flying first class when the nonprofit's policy restricts travel to coach fares only). In addition, a nonprofit board member should demonstrate unselfish loyalty to the organization and avoid any conflict — or appearance thereof — between the organization's interests and those of the board member.

Claims alleging breach of the duty of loyalty are common in suits filed against nonprofit boards. Examples of the types of claims that might assert violation of the *duty of loyalty* include:

■   A board member of a nonprofit community development agency receives a finder's fee for securing financing for an upcoming project.

■   A board member discloses to a third party confidential information he learned of during a board meeting.

■   The treasurer of a nonprofit board borrows money from the organization's endowment fund for personal use.

2.  The **duty of care** requires that board members use diligence in governing the organization. This duty is often interpreted as applying the care that an ordinarily prudent person would use under similar circumstances.

From a practical standpoint, the courts have granted boards a great deal of latitude in conducting the affairs of their organizations. Through the application of the "business judgment rule," directors and officers are immune from personal liability for mistakes attributed to business judgment. The applicability of this protection assumes that no illegal conduct takes place and that the director acts responsibly. Interpretations include regularly attending and participating in meetings, and staying abreast of the organization's affairs. In order to fulfill the duty of care nonprofit boards must be proactive — for example, implement programs and safeguards that promote appropriate conduct and detect and address inappropriate conduct. Two areas requiring special attention are fundraising and financial management. A board fulfilling the duty of care makes certain that the nonprofit's fundraising activities further the organization's mission and that costs are reasonable when compared to the amount raised. The prudent board also manages investments wisely and carefully weighs reasonable rates of return against investment risks.

Examples of the types of claims that might allege breach of the *duty of care* include:

- A suit by a former employee alleging sexual harassment and the board's negligent oversight of the nonprofit's operations.

- The association's headquarters has fallen into disrepair and the building has been condemned by the local building inspector. Members of the association bring an action against the board alleging negligent waste of charitable assets.

3.   The **duty of obedience** requires that a board member act only within the scope of the powers granted by law or the nonprofit's charter, articles of incorporation, and bylaws. *Ultra vires* actions are those that fall outside the scope of a board member's authority. An individual board member or the entire board if appropriate, can be held personally responsible for *ultra vires* acts. The common law duty of obedience also requires that the board adopt and follow conduct protocols, or rules and procedures that govern its actions. Examples of board protocols include rules

concerning the number of meetings held each year, board meeting minutes, and filing of reports required by regulators. Failure to establish and follow board protocol may defeat the protection afforded by the "corporate veil," and lead to personal liability for the results.

Examples of the types of activities that might generate claims alleging breach of the *duty of obedience* include:

- At the end of the fiscal year, the board votes to distribute net income for the year to any or all directors.

- Because of busy travel schedules and the relative lack of organization activity, the board agrees to forego two of the four board meetings scheduled for the year. Consequently, the board's inattention and violation of its bylaws resulted in the nonprofit ceasing operations. The state attorney general begins an investigation into the operation of the organization.

## B. Pursue a Multi-Faceted Strategy

As community-serving nonprofits grow and many assume responsibility for social services previously delivered by governments, the need for committed, enthusiastic, and capable volunteer board members has never been greater. While claims against nonprofit boards remain rare — most nonprofits will never be sued in their institutional lifetimes — the fear of liability continues to grow. This fear is fueled, in part, by widespread publicity surrounding celebrated cases. This publicity in turn leads to more claims. Nonprofit and corporate directors share a common concern: that of personal liability for serving on a board. At the end of litigation against nonprofits, nonprofit board members are rarely required to use personal funds to pay for harm committed by the board or organization, but the possibility remains. Some party or the nonprofit itself may charge the director with a breach of duty that he or she owed to that party.

Every nonprofit must work diligently to recruit and retain suitable board leaders. One strategy is to address the potential for personal liability by taking steps that substantially reduce the likelihood that a board member's personal assets will be exposed to loss. We suggest a three-part protection strategy for nonprofit boards as described below:

1. **Risk Control** — Every nonprofit should begin the process of reducing the potential of a director being held personally responsible by minimizing the risk. This effort begins with examining the board's governance activities, and the common law duties owed by each and every board member. Do board members fully understand their legal duties? Do board operations reflect a commitment to fulfill these duties? What actions are taken when a breach of a fiduciary duty is suspected? Has the board established rules and procedures governing its operations? Are these procedures followed?

The process of identifying priority risks and implementing strategies to address them should continue with all major operational areas. Form a volunteer risk management committee to coordinate the process of risk identification and strategy development. Even the smallest nonprofit can and should establish a risk management committee. In smaller nonprofits volunteers will hold most of the seats on the committee, while in a midsize or large nonprofit the committee may consist principally of paid staff. The nonprofit should focus first on high priority risks — those most likely to occur and those with the greatest financial and other adverse impact on the organization.

2. **Indemnification & Volunteer Protection** — Most nonprofit bylaws include indemnification provisions — language that expresses the intent of the nonprofit to cover the expenses a board member might incur in defending an action and paying settlements or judgments related to his service on the board. There are circumstances, however, when indemnification is not available or becomes a hollow promise. These include:

■ When the nonprofit does not have sufficient resources to pay the losses and expenses incurred by a director or officer;

- When state or federal law limits the protection that may be afforded through indemnification due to public policy considerations;

- When the board is unsympathetic to the plight of the director who has been sued and refuses to authorize the indemnification;

- When the organization decides that it is inappropriate to use the nonprofit's financial resources to indemnify a director.

Every state has a volunteer protection law and the federal Volunteer Protection Act (VPA) became the law of the land in September 1997. The Volunteer Protection Act provides that, if a volunteer meets certain criteria, he or she shall not be liable for simple negligence while acting on behalf of a nonprofit or governmental organization. The VPA also provides some limitations on the assessment of noneconomic losses and punitive damages against a volunteer. The Volunteer Protection Act does not, however, protect a volunteer from liability for harm "caused by willful or criminal misconduct, gross negligence, reckless misconduct, or a conscious, flagrant indifference to the rights or safety of the individual harmed by the volunteer action." The Act does not *prohibit* lawsuits against volunteers nor does it provide any protection for nonprofits (see Appendix B, Frequently Asked Questions About D&O for additional information on the VPA).

The state volunteer liability laws vary significantly. Some states only protect directors and officers while other states extend the protection to all volunteers, however, every volunteer protection statute has exceptions. The most common exclusions are for claims based on a volunteer's willful or wanton misconduct, criminal acts, or self-dealing.

3. **Risk Financing** — Every nonprofit must consider how it will pay for injuries, damages, legal expenses and other costs that stem from the harm it causes. For some organizations, reserve funds are sufficient to pay for anticipated losses. For the majority of the nation's 1.5 million nonprofits, reserves are inadequate. For this reason, a

growing number of nonprofits choose to purchase insurance and pay an annual premium in exchange for the promise that funds will be available in the event a covered loss occurs.

## C. Exercise Diligence and Caution

As we indicated at the start of this book, the most effective risk management strategy is the one that avoids a loss. Financing potential claims — through the purchase of D&O coverage or some other means — should be approached only after you have first tried to minimize the likelihood of claims. Remember, however, that no strategy can eliminate the possibility... virtually anyone can sue your nonprofit at any time for almost any reason.

The suggestions below are a starting point for minimizing governance risks in your nonprofit. For information on developing a comprehensive risk management program, see *Mission Accomplished: A Practical Guide to Risk Management for Nonprofits*, available from the Nonprofit Risk Management Center.

1. *Make certain your board knows its legal responsibilities.* A nonprofit board cannot be expected to fulfill duties that it is unaware of. Conduct an annual board orientation for new members that includes an explanation of the legal duties of loyalty, care, and obedience.

2. *Recognize that the board has overall responsibility for the employment practices of the nonprofit.* This does not mean that the board should be involved in day-to-day personnel decisions. Rather, the board should develop (with assistance from an employment attorney) and adopt employment policies (typically compiled in an employee handbook or personnel policies manual), review periodically the employment policies of the nonprofit, and ask questions when any board member has concerns about exposure to employment liability claims. Employment practices liability (EPL) claims represent an estimated 75 percent of all claims filed under nonprofit D&O policies. The board should pay particular attention to policies pertaining to termination and

discharge, since wrongful termination claims account for 60 percent of all employment practices claims. Always consult an experienced employment attorney before adopting any new employment policies or changing existing policies.

3. *Take care to follow established policies and abolish those that no longer meet the needs of the nonprofit.* A nonprofit organization or board of directors that fails to follow the rules and procedures it has established is at risk. All policies should be administered fairly and consistently. Consult a qualified legal advisor before adopting new operational policies.

4. *Establish a risk management committee to avoid being reactive to losses.* The committee should be dedicated to scanning the horizon for possible harm caused by the nonprofit's activities and developing prevention strategies.

5. *Establish and follow a formal policy concerning conflicts of interest.* Nonprofits and their governing boards can come under fire for even the appearance of a conflict of interest. The public's support and that of your donors and volunteers is too important to risk allegations of impropriety. Recognize that operating a nonprofit means adhering to special rules that protect the public's interest. Board members should be cautious about entering into business relationships with the nonprofits they serve, and a board should be cautious about allowing such a relationship to occur. These transactions should not occur unless the board determines it is clearly in the best interest of the nonprofit. The conflict of interest policy should include a procedure for annual written disclosure by all board members of their business activities with the nonprofit and their other board memberships.

6. *Encourage rigorous review of charitable programs and services.* Don't allow the  board to blindly accept every proposal presented by staff. A board that is fulfilling its legal duties questions proposed activities and is diligent in protecting and preserving the trust afforded the nonprofit by virtue of its corporate status. A board that simply rubber stamps staff proposals should not be allowed to continue.

Every board should use its own judgment and not simply take the word of the CEO.

7. ***Secure independent professional advisors.*** Many start-up boards rely on their own members for legal, accounting, and insurance advice. As soon as practicably possible, every nonprofit should secure independent professional advisors, including an attorney, an auditor/CPA, and an insurance broker, agent or advisor.

8. ***Require the regular scrutiny of the nonprofit's financial statements and pay close attention to other financial matters.*** The full board should review the nonprofit's financial statements on a quarterly basis. More frequent review by the Finance Committee is also appropriate. If it appears that board members do not understand the financial statements, provide a training session. The board of directors should also: review and adopt realistic annual budgets, ensure that the nonprofit has adequate internal accounting/financial management systems, request periodic confirmation that required filings are up-to-date, make certain that fees charged by professional fundraisers are reasonable, and ensure that restricted contributions are used in accordance with the donor's requirements.

9. ***Require regular attendance and encourage full participation.*** As indicated previously, board members have a legal duty to stay up-to-date on the affairs of the nonprofit. Ignorance is neither an excuse nor a defense. Board members cannot make informed decisions about critical matters without background materials provided in advance of board meetings allowing sufficient time for a thorough review. The minutes of board meetings should reflect the discussion as well as the final decision on substantive matters.

10. ***Conduct an annual review of the CEO and a self-assessment of the board's performance.*** One of the board's principal responsibilities is to oversee the delegation of daily operations, more specifically, the performance of the nonprofit's chief executive officer. The main purpose is to help the CEO perform more effectively and thereby enable

the nonprofit to achieve its mission. Perhaps equally important is the board's review of its own performance. The board should examine how it is meeting its responsibilities and duties. Some elements to consider are the composition of its membership, individual members' performance, its selection process, and compliance with the organization's bylaws and mission. This exercise is also a good reminder for all board members of what the organization should be striving to achieve under their guidance.

# Chapter 3
# Background on D&O Insurance

## A. History of D&O

*P*rior to the early 1960s, overseas insurers such as Lloyd's of London were the only writers of directors' and officers' policies for for-profit entities. In the 1960s, two major US companies, St. Paul and American International Group (AIG), began writing corporate D&O policies. The number of policies sold grew considerably after 1968 when Delaware (as a leading state for corporate domiciles) passed new laws authorizing corporations to purchase D&O liability coverage.

Today, several dozen US-based insurers sell the vast majority of D&O coverage for businesses and nonprofits. Besides the number of companies, each insurer offers many different "forms," including in some cases, one or more policies written specifically for nonprofits. Therefore, D&O policy language and coverage differs from one form to the next. Insurance companies then further complicate D&O policies by attaching endorsements that modify coverages. A D&O policy can have ten or more endorsements that the insured must review and attempt to understand.

> Throughout this chapter, we reference actual policy forms to illustrate various points. Some of these forms may not be currently available from the insurers cited. In other cases, the insurers may have undergone some reorganization and may no longer operate under the name noted.

## B. Must We Purchase D&O Coverage?

State laws permit — but do not require — the purchase of directors' and officers' liability coverage by a nonprofit organization. There are, however, various volunteer protection statutes at the state level whose terms are affected by whether a nonprofit maintains liability coverage of a prescribed amount. For example, under a number of state volunteer protection statutes immunity for simple negligence by a volunteer is contingent upon the nonprofit organization's purchase of liability insurance with a specified limit. This means that a volunteer working for a nonprofit without insurance is vulnerable to claims, even those alleging simple negligence.

Under a D&O insurance policy, coverage is provided for the defense of actual or alleged "wrongful acts" taken by directors, officers, and other "insureds" under the policy. As indicated previously, the person filing suit may be an insider such as an employee or volunteer, or an outsider, such as a service recipient, donor, or government official.

While directors' and officers' liability insurance may provide defense against allegations of fraudulent, criminal or dishonest acts, these acts are not insurable (nor indemnifiable) as a matter of public policy. However, many policies amend the exclusion so that it only applies when a final adjudication establishes such acts. Final adjudication means that the directors or officers have been found liable by a court. The wording of this exclusion will vary by policy and does not always rely upon a court finding.

Every nonprofit must decide for itself whether or not it should purchase D&O insurance. As mentioned earlier, the agency's indemnification agreement for the board members is only as good as the financial resources available to fund the indemnification. Some wrongful acts are neither insurable nor indemnifiable, however the vast majority of allegations against the board, staff, and the organization will be activities potentially covered by a D&O policy. We discuss the various coverages and limitations of D&O policies in the next section. This information will help you assess your need for D&O insurance.

## C. Sources of Claims Against Nonprofit Boards

One of the myths associated with nonprofit D&O exposures is that there are few sources of claims since nonprofits do not have shareholders. Nonprofits serve large and varied constituencies to which their boards owe specific fiduciary duties similar to duties owed by corporate boards. These constituencies are potential plaintiffs in legal actions brought against nonprofit boards. Potential claimants in a suit against nonprofit directors include:

1. ***Insiders.*** The current and former staff of a nonprofit may bring actions alleging a host of wrongful acts, including wrongful termination, discrimination, sexual harassment, Americans with Disabilities Act violations, and more.

2. ***Outsiders.*** Third parties that have a relationship with the nonprofit may allege harm caused by the nonprofit and/or its directors, officers or employees. Outside sources can be vendors, funders, and another nonprofit.

3. ***The Entity.*** The nonprofit may bring an action against its directors and officers. Examples include claims by current management against a former trustee. In some states, derivative suits are permitted. In a derivative suit, members of a nonprofit may bring a claim on the nonprofit's behalf against a director and officer. (Note: Claims by the entity against its directors and officers will likely be excluded under most nonprofit D&O policies).

4. ***Directors.*** A nonprofit director may sue another board member alleging violation of a duty owed to the nonprofit. Under certain circumstances such an action may be compelled.

5. ***Beneficiaries.*** The people you are in business to help — your service recipients — may bring claims against directors and officers alleging wrongdoing.

6. ***Members.*** Directors and officers of membership associations are vulnerable to claims brought by members alleging harm to the interests of the member.

7. **Donors.** A nonprofit's contributors may sue directors and officers alleging misuse of a restricted gift.

8. **State Attorney General.** In most states, the state attorney general represents the interests of the general public in assuring the proper management of public benefit corporations. As such, the Attorney General may bring a claim against nonprofit directors and officers alleging wrongdoing.

9. **Other Government Officials.** Other government officials, including representatives of the Internal Revenue Service and the Department of Labor, may bring actions against nonprofit directors alleging violation of state or federal laws.

# Chapter 4
# About the D&O Policy

## A. The Application

*H*appily, simplification is the trend in nonprofit D&O
application forms. At least one insurer has adopted a
one-page application for a particular policy offered to
nonprofits with annual budgets under $200,000.

Having said that, most nonprofit D&O coverages are
underwritten (the process of determining whether coverage
will be offered, what policy provisions will be included, and
at what price) principally on the basis of the information
contained in the insurance application and various required
attachments. Most D&O insurers request some or all of the
following: a copy of the board roster; current financial
statements, most recent audited financial statements, or
Form 990; and the employee handbook or personnel policies
manual. Because it forms the basis for the carrier's decision
to provide coverage, the application itself (and in most cases,
other required attachments) becomes a part of the insurance
contract. Therefore, the policies contain a provision that the
insured represents that the application is true, accurate and
complete and that the application is incorporated into the
policy. Any material untruth, misrepresentation or omission
in the application will void the policy for the insureds
responsible for or having the benefit of such knowledge.

D&O applications generally contain a warranty located just above the space for a signature. For example:

> "The undersigned being authorized by, and acting on behalf of, the applicant and all persons or concerns seeking insurance, has read and understands this application, and declares all statements set forth herein are true, complete and accurate. The undersigned further declares and represents that any occurrence or event taking place prior to the inception of the policy applied for, which may render inaccurate, untrue, or incomplete any statement made herein, will immediately be reported in writing to the insurer. The undersigned acknowledges and agrees that the submission and the insurer's receipt of such report, prior to the inception of the policy applied for, is a condition precedent to coverage.

> "The signing of this application does not bind the undersigned to purchase the insurance, nor does review of the application bind the insurance company to issue a policy. It is agreed that this application shall be the basis of the contract should a policy be issued."

> — *Coregis, SOR.OOC 1902 (4/97)*

An important concern is that a misrepresentation by the person completing the application could void coverage for everyone intended as an insured, including the nonprofit, individual board members, other volunteers, and employees. It is unlikely that members of a nonprofit board or more than a single staff member will be involved in completing an application. Despite this fact, courts have upheld recision of policies where an officer signing the application made a misrepresentation unknown to other insureds *(Bird v. Penn Central Co.*, 334 F. Supp. 255 (E.D. Pa. 1972) and *Shapiro v. American Home Assurance Co.*, 584 F. Supp. 1245 (D. Mass. 1984). Perhaps in response to these outcomes, most nonprofit D&O policies contain a *severability clause* that preserves coverage for any insured that is unaware of misstatements and misrepresentations made by other insureds on the application for coverage. The severability clause ensures that knowledge of false statements on the application is not imputed (transferred) to other insureds.

The policy language may read:

> "In issuing this policy, the company has relied on the declarations and statements which are contained in the application and which are deemed to be incorporated in this policy, provided, however, that except for material circumstances known to the person who subscribed the application, any misstatement or omission in such application in respect of a specific WRONGFUL ACT by a particular INSURED or his cognizance of any manner which he has reason to suppose might afford grounds for a future CLAIM against him shall not be imputed to any other INSURED for the purpose of determining the availability of coverage under this policy."
>
> — *Coregis, CFM 93.1.0494 (8/93)*

Material misstatements on the application can result in the denial of coverage for specific types of claims, the denial of coverage for certain insureds, or the recision of the policy altogether. As a result, the application should be carefully completed by the person in the best position to respond. If you are uncertain about a question on the application, ask your insurance advisor to explain the question.

## B. Written to Confuse?

Many nonprofit insurance buyers get frustrated easily by the complexity of insurance contract language. It is a frustration shared by those in and outside the industry, including a federal court that wrote:

> "This case presents another illustration of the dangers of the present complex structuring of insurance policies. Unfortunately the insurance industry has become addicted to the practice of building into policies one condition or exception upon another in the shape of a linguistic Tower of Babel... We reiterate our plea for clarity and simplicity in policies that fulfill so important a public service." – Wilson, J., in *Keating v. National Union Fire Insurance Co.*, No. CV89-5343, C.D. Cal, May 19, 1990.

Today insurance companies write nonprofit D&O policies in a variety of ways. Some carriers offer a "for-profit" D&O

policy with additional coverages provided through endorsements to modify coverage for nonprofits. In this example, the main policy provides minimal coverage to "corporate" directors with substantive exclusions, and the nonprofit coverages are restored through various endorsements that modify the provisions in the main policy. Another choice for the nonprofit buyer is a policy form that is designed for nonprofit organizations and provides the essential coverages. These policies may be called "Nonprofit Organization Liability Insurance," "Not-for-Profit Organization Professional Liability Insurance," or something similar.

There are also varying structures used by insurance companies to craft policy language that can be either specific or nonspecific. In a policy that provides specific coverage, the insurer's intent is clear. For example, "We shall pay any premium on appeal bonds for the covered part of a judgment." The other form of policy construction emphasizes what the policy does not cover. The interpretation is that the policy covers everything not specifically excluded.

Under the doctrine of *contra proferentem*, when a term in an insurance policy is ambiguous, the courts construe the policy language in favor of providing coverage for the policyholder. Some insurance advisors argue that a vaguely worded or "open-ended" policy is inherently better because it provides broader coverage than a specific one.

However, the broad form may be worrisome to nonprofit buyers. One cannot be certain if coverage will be provided until a coverage trigger occurs — a claim is made against the policy. Some insurance advisors warn against seeking an "underwriting opinion" on a hypothetical claim. First, the opinion is only for a hypothetical claim — every claim is different and the actual claim may vary substantially from the scenario you imagined. Second, it is not the underwriter that pays the claim, but the claims department. Unfortunately, underwriting and claims departments do not always agree. Sometimes there is a disagreement between the insurance company and the insured regarding coverage. If the insurer denies coverage, the insured can sue the company to seek resolution. Unfortunately, the cost of this litigation is high on both sides. Insurance companies spend over $1 billion annually to fund litigation battles against their policyholders.

Other insurance advisors believe that under certain circumstances, an underwriting opinion can be very helpful. For example, when a policy is silent on an issue such as "certification," an exchange of correspondence between the insured, broker, and carrier can be helpful in determining the carrier's intent. In some cases, underwriters have significant input in claims decisions and in fact are active participants in claims committee meetings.

## C. D&O Coverage Elements

Now that you understand the role of insurance in a risk management program and ways to reduce your D&O exposure, you are ready to consider the various features of nonprofit D&O policies.

In the pages that follow, we discuss specific coverage areas in detail. Our intent is to explain how and why these coverages may be important to your nonprofit. Every nonprofit's exposures are unique. As a result, the appropriate risk financing strategy for each nonprofit may also be different. It is impossible and inappropriate to outline the policy provisions that would be suitable for every nonprofit. Each buyer — whether a senior manager or a committee of volunteers — must match the purchased coverage to the exposures it seeks to finance. As you read each section, consider whether the described provision is important to your nonprofit. Use what you have learned from this book to discuss your coverage needs and preferences with your insurance agent or broker.

More than ever before, a nonprofit seeking D&O insurance has many choices. Currently, the insurance marketplace is highly competitive — longtime players are selling enhanced coverages to an expanding nonprofit customer base and emerging players in the nonprofit D&O market are setting ambitious production goals. Many companies offer user-friendly policies, some have developed special forms and pricing for smaller nonprofits, and all have simplified application forms. Major insurance carriers are well aware that the charitable sector is the fastest growing component of our economy. This is a mixed blessing when purchasing insurance coverage. The process is easier because you should not have to look far for competitive coverage and reasonable premiums. But it is also more difficult because the substantial differences in coverage require a thorough review of policy wording. The following sections provide explanations and guidance in reviewing D&O insurance policy language.

1) **Claims-Made**

Directors' and officers' liability insurance policies are written on a claims-made basis. With a claims-made policy, coverage is triggered based on when the claim is made, not when the incident giving rise to the claim occurred.

For example, a nonprofit has a D&O policy running from 1/1/98 to 1/1/99. The nonprofit terminates an employee in November of 1997. The terminated employee sues the nonprofit in February of 1998 alleging age discrimination and wrongful termination. A claims-made form would respond because the claim (lawsuit) was made during the policy period, despite the fact that the alleged wrongful act (the termination) occurred before the policy period.

It is critical for the insured to report claims to the insurance company as soon as possible. In addition to a notation on the declarations page, the policy's insuring agreement identifies the policy as providing claims-made coverage. Typical wording is as follows:

> 1. The Company will pay on behalf of an **Insured** all **Loss** which such **Insured** becomes legally obligated to pay on account of any **Claim** first made against such **Insured** during the **Policy Period** or, if exercised, during the Extended Reporting Period, for:

a. a **Wrongful Act,**

b. **Employment Practices,** or

c. **Personal Injury** or **Publishers Liability**

Committed, attempted, or allegedly committed or attempted, by such **Insured** before or during the **Policy Period**.

*— Chubb, Form 14-02-2009 (Ed. 5-96)*

In most D&O policies the claim must be made *and* reported to the insurance company during the policy period. Therefore, it is important to understand first how the policy defines a claim and secondly, what your requirements are for reporting the claim to the insurance company. Timely reporting is also critical. Many nonprofits have gotten into trouble when they have tried to defend a claim on their own and only report it to an insurer once the situation has gotten out of hand.

2) **Definition of "Claim"**

As mentioned above, defining a "claim" is important because coverage is only triggered when you report a claim properly to the insurance company. In addition to defining the word "claim," D&O policies have very specific requirements for reporting claims to the company. The improper or late reporting of a claim can negate coverage.

The definition of claim involves two parts, notice and coverage. A few policies only define claim in relation to the notice given to the insured and company and rely on other sections of the policy to describe the coverage.

For example:

(C) "**Claim**" means written notice received by an **Insured** that any person or entity intends to hold any **Insured** responsible for a **Wrongful Act**. A **Claim** will be deemed to have been made when such written notice is first received by any **Insured**.

*— Executive Risk Indemnity Inc., Form C22208 (9/96 ed.)*

Equally important is the policy's requirements for reporting a claim to the insurance company. If the nonprofit does not report the claim or potential claim correctly, there might not be coverage. Most policies require written notice to the insurer and some even specify where the notice is to be sent. Look for headings entitled "Notice" or "Reporting and Notice" to determine your policy's requirements. Here is typical wording:

REPORTING AND NOTICE

4.1  A specific **Wrongful Act** shall be considered to have been first reported to the Company:

(A)  at the time that any **Insured** first gives written notice to the Company that a claim has been made against the **Insured** for such **Wrongful Act**; or

(B)  at the time that any **Insured** first gives written notice to the Company (1) of the material facts or circumstances relating to such **Wrongful Act** as facts and circumstances having the potential of giving rise to a claim being made against the **Insured** or (2) of the receipt of written or oral notice from any party that it is the intention of such party to hold the **Insured** responsible for such **Wrongful Act**;

whichever occurs first.

4.2  The **Insured** shall, as a condition precedent to their rights under this policy, give the Company written notice as soon as practicable of any claim made against any of them for a **Wrongful Act** and shall give the Company such information and cooperation as it may reasonably require.

— *Chubb, Form 14-02-284 (Ed. 1-82)*

The next consideration is how the insurance company defines claim and its coverage. Some nonprofit D&O policies provide broad coverage for a wide range of claims while others restrict coverage to "claims for money damages." A growing number of policies provide coverage for any demand, suit, or proceeding including judicial, administrative or regulatory. The claim can be for monetary damages, services, or equitable or other relief. The value of including proceedings as a claim is that the policy will respond to such actions as complaints filed with local human rights commissions or the Equal Employment Opportunity Commission (EEOC). Under a policy that provides such coverage the definition of "claim" may include language such as *Claim means a civil, criminal, or administrative adjudicatory proceeding initiated against the Insured*, or demand for money damages." Many nonprofits represent their organizations at such hearings without the benefit of counsel. Others use *pro bono* or retained counsel to assist in preparing for these proceedings.

Usually if the nonprofit does not notify the insurance company of the filing and hearing, its expenses will not be credited towards its policy deductible or retention. Occasionally, an insurer will provide defense counsel for an administrative proceeding even though the policy does not include that in its definition of claim. An insurer will do so because it believes that it is in the company's economic interest to resolve the matter at an early stage. Some insurance companies recognize that a finding against the nonprofit at the commission level can lead to a costly civil lawsuit later.

The key point is to know what your policy covers. If the policy's definition of claim is narrow — "demand for compensatory damages," "demand for monetary damages" or "civil lawsuit" — then you know that you may be on your own at an administrative or other proceeding. If your policy provides coverage for administrative proceedings, remember that you need to report any EEOC complaints or notices to appear at administrative hearings to your insurer. Beware that the definition of claim is not the only place in the policy where the company details its responsibilities. One policy we examined had a broad definition of "claim," but then narrowed coverage by excluding liability for any "Claims... in any form other than money damages..."

For example:

> "Claim means any demand for compensatory damages, whether formal or informal, written or oral, as a result of a WRONGFUL ACT. CLAIM does not mean, nor shall this Policy

respond to, requests or demands for other than compensatory damages."

— *Coregis, COR.OOC.2043 (7/97)*

"This policy does not apply to:

I.    Any claim alleging, based upon or arising out of claims, demands or actions seeking relief or redress in any form other than money damages, or for claimant/plaintiff attorney fees or expenses relating to claims, demands or actions seeking relief or redress in any form other than money damages."

— *Coregis, CFM 93.1.0494 (8/93)*

Note:  the policies cited above provide coverage for nonmonetary complaints via endorsement.

An example of a broadly worded definition:

"Claim" means:

1.    a civil, criminal, or administrative adjudicatory proceeding, or

2.    a written demand for monetary damages, against the Insureds for a Wrongful Act, including any appeal therefrom.

— *CNA G-20717-A (ED. 2/94)*

The broadest form of coverage responds to all claims or demands for damages without specifying that the insured receive "written notice of a claim."

Another consideration in reviewing the coverage for a "claim," is the policy's definition of loss. Loss usually means damages, judgments, settlements, and defense costs that are subject to certain exclusions. Many policies exclude coverage for punitive or exemplary damages and fines, taxes or penalties.

For example:

"**Loss**" means damages, judgments, settlements or other amounts which an insured is obligated to pay as a result of a **Claim**. "**Loss**" will not, however, include:

1) fines, taxes or penalties, punitive or exemplary damages or the multiplied portion of any multiplied damage award;

2) fees or other charges of any **Insured**, including but not limited to salaries, overhead or benefit expenses of any **Insured**;

3) any amount which an **Insured** is obligated to pay as a result of any portion of a **Claim** seeking relief or redress in any form other than money damages; or

4) any salary, wages or other employment-related benefits which an **Insured** is obligated to pay (a) to an employee under an express written contract (i) to commence or continue employment or (ii) to make any payment in the event of termination of employment, or (b) by operation of the Fair Labor Standards Act, the National Labor Relations Act, ..., other similar provisions of any federal, state, or local statutory or common law or any rules or regulations promulgated under any of the foregoing.

— *Executive Risk Indemnity Inc., C22208 (9/96 ed.)*

In rare instances, the D&O policy does not define the term *claim*. In such cases, claim usually means any demand for damages and other relief. However, review the remaining policy language to determine how *claim* and *loss* may be interpreted or defined.

3) **Prior Acts Coverage**

In order to understand the provisions of prior acts coverage, you need to know how a claims-made policy works. Under a claims-made policy, the claim must be made, filed, or charged during the policy period — regardless of when the incident giving rise to the claim occurred. The next step is to define what is a "claim" under your policy. If the incident seems to meet the definition, review the policy's requirements for reporting a claim. Most policies require you to provide written notice "as soon as practicable after it is first made." In addition, most policies contain a provision permitting the insured to give written notice to the company of any potential claims.

For example:

> (2)  If, during the **Policy Period**, an **Insured** first becomes aware of a **Wrongful Act** which may subsequently give rise to a **Claim** and, as soon as practicable thereafter but before the end of the **Policy Period**:
>
> (a)  gives the Underwriter written notice of such **Wrongful Act**, ...
>
> (b)  requests coverage under this Policy for any subsequently resulting **Claim** for such **Wrongful Act**;
>
> the Underwriter will treat any such subsequent **Claim** as if it had been first made during the **Policy Year** in which such notice was given.
>
> — *Executive Risk Indemnity Inc., Form C22208 (9/96 ed.)*

Some policies provide specific direction on when claims must be reported, such as within two weeks or one month after the claim is made.

The next issue is whether or not the policy covers any known "prior acts" that occurred prior to the policy inception. D&O policies exclude coverage for any claims that the organization knew about or had already received notice. The reason for this exclusion is that few insurance companies want to cover an existing claim or loss. The theory is that an insured would only be motivated to purchase insurance after they knew of a loss and adversely select against the insurance company.

A sample of a known prior acts exclusion follows:

> The company will not cover claims which are:
>
> D.  based upon, directly or indirectly arising out of, or in any way involving:
>
> 1.  any **Wrongful Act** or any manner, fact, circumstance, situation, transaction, or event which has been the subject of any claim made prior to the effective date of this Policy or of any notice given during any prior policy of which this policy is a successor; or

2. any **Wrongful Act** whenever occurring, which, together with a **Wrongful Act** which has been the subject of such claim or such notice, would constitute **Interrelated Wrongful Acts**;

F. based upon, directly or indirectly arising out of, or in any way involving any civil, criminal or administrative proceeding prior to or pending on the date set forth in Item 8. of the Declarations, or any fact, circumstance, situation, transaction or event underlying or alleged in such proceeding.

— CNA, G-20717-A (ED. 2/94)

Note that these exclusions apply to claims or potential claims that are "known" to the insured. This raises the issue of who within the organization is charged with the responsibility to know and report potential and actual claims. Most policies offer a severability clause that usually pertains to the application but may extend to future claims. The clause may read: ". . . no statement in the application or knowledge possessed by any **Insured** shall be imputed to any other **Insured** for the purpose of determining the availability of coverage with respect to claims made against any **Insured** whether or not the Association grants indemnification." (Chubb, Form 14-02-284 Ed. 1-82).

Another potential coverage problem exists if the policy contains a "retroactive date." A retroactive date specifies how far into the past the policy extends coverage for prior acts. Therefore, if the incident occurred before the retroactive date and although the claim was first made after the policy's retroactive date, the policy would not respond to the claim. A policy with a retroactive date does not provide coverage for "full prior acts."

Another feature to look for is a clause in the policy that requires that the wrongful act and claim reporting occur during the policy period. This is a very stringent condition that may be difficult to honor. If you purchase continuous coverage from the same carrier or prior acts coverage, the policy period may be longer than a year, and extend back to the first date on which you purchased continuously in force coverage.

## 4) **Entity Coverage**

Historically, the insurance industry developed D&O policies to cover specifically the directors and officers of a corporation, not the corporation itself. Today, companies have modified their forms from the early models. Unfortunately, many contain vestiges of the old that are no longer appropriate. The best example is the lack of *entity coverage*. Entity coverage ensures that the policy coverage extends to the organization (a legal entity) as well as the directors, officers and others. Under a policy that provides entity coverage, the nonprofit may be called the "Insured Entity," "Organization," "Association," or even simply the "Entity."

Entity coverage is probably crucial for your nonprofit. First, your nonprofit is a likely target in litigation brought by a disgruntled employee, service recipient, or outsider. It is also possible that only the nonprofit — and not individual directors — will be named. If this were to happen in a policy limiting coverage to directors and officers, no coverage would be provided for the lawsuit. Many suits name multiple defendants. For example, in a suit brought by a former employee named defendants could include the nonprofit, the CEO, a supervisor, and the board of directors. Without the entity coverage, the insurance company may still defend the organization if named. However, the company might then allocate the costs between the insured directors and officers and the uninsured nonprofit and seek reimbursement from the nonprofit for its defense costs.

Read your policy carefully to determine whether entity coverage is provided. The first place to look is the policy's Insuring Agreements.

For example:

"Insured" means the Organization and the Insured Person(s)."

— *National Union Fire Insurance Company of Pittsburgh, PA, 49363 (12/89)*

In the above policy, the policy title "New York Non-For-Profit Organization/Directors and Officers Liability Policy" suggests entity coverage.

Another definition of insured provides:

> "Insured(s) means the ENTITY named in the Declarations and any individual who was..."
>
> — *Coregis, CFM 93.1.0494 (8/93)*

## 5) **Definition of Insured**

Some D&O policies, especially "for-profit" forms, contain a narrow definition of "insured" — limiting coverage to *current* directors and officers of the organization. A more extensive policy will contain a broad definition of insured. The definition may provide coverage for the nonprofit (the entity or organization) and all past, present, and future directors, officers, trustees, employees, committee members, and volunteers. A savvy plaintiff's attorney will likely name everyone connected to the event or decision in a suit alleging injury. A broad definition of insured offers protection to named defendants that falls outside the narrow definition of "director" or "officer."

For example,

> "Insured Person means any natural person who has been, now is or shall become a duly elected director or trustee, duly elected or appointed officer, employee or committee member (whether or not salaried) of an Organization, and any natural person acting in a voluntary capacity on behalf of an Organization and at the specific direction of such Organization."
>
> — *Chubb, Form 14-02-2009 (Ed.0596)*

> "INSURED(S) means the ENTITY named in the Declarations and any person, while acting within the scope of his or her duties and responsibilities for the ENTITY, who was, now is, or shall be a director, officer, trustee, employee, volunteer, or staff member of the ENTITY, and shall include any executive, board member or committee member, whether salaried or not. INSURED shall also include the estates of, and lawful

spouses of, individual INSUREDS as defined above, for CLAIMS against an estate or marital estate arising out of WRONGFUL ACTS by such individual insured.

*— Coregis, COR.OOC.2043 (7/97)*

### 6) Definition of "Wrongful Act"

Another important definition in determining policy coverage is "wrongful act." The definitions vary and are significant because the "wrongful act" is the primary component of the policy's insuring agreement.

For example:

"Wrongful Act means any error, misstatement or misleading statement, act or omission, or neglect or breach of duty committed, attempted or allegedly committed or attempted by an Insured individually or otherwise, in the discharge of his duties to the Association, or any matter claimed against him solely by reason of his serving in such capacity. All such causally connected errors, statements, acts, omissions, neglects or breaches of duty of other such matters committed or attempted by, allegedly committed or attempted by or claimed against one or more of the Insureds shall be deemed interrelated Wrongful Acts."

*— Chubb, Form 14-02-284 (Ed. 1-82)*

"WRONGFUL ACT means any actual or alleged error or omission, negligent act, misleading statement, or breach of duty committed by an INSURED in the performance of duties on behalf of the ENTITY."

*— Coregis, COR.OOC.2043 (7/97)*

"Wrongful Act" means any breach of duty, error, neglect, omission or act committed solely in the course of the activities of the Organization, including but not limited to:

1.   false arrest, wrongful detention or imprisonment, or malicious prosecution;

2.   libel, slander, defamation of character, or invasion of privacy;

3.   wrongful entry, eviction or other invasion of the right of privacy;

4.   infringement of copyright or trademark or unauthorized use of title;

5.   plagiarism or misappropriation of ideas;

6.   Claims, arising from employment practices relating to a past, present or prospective employee of the Organization, including but not limited to, any actual or alleged wrongful termination, either actual or constructive; wrongful failure to employ or promote; wrongful deprivation of career opportunity; wrongful discipline; alleged unlawful discrimination as defined by Title VII and/or the Unruh Civil Rights Act, whether direct, indirect, intentional or unintentional; or failure to provide adequate employee policies and procedures.

All damages involving the same Wrongful Act or a series of continuous or interrelated Wrongful Acts will be considered as arising out of one Wrongful Act."

*— NIAC DO (7/98)*

In certain policies the definition of "wrongful act" is open-ended. Insurance advisors may argue that this form of construction works to the Insured's benefit if a potential claim does not fit within a prescriptive definition of claim.

For example,

"Wrongful Act" means any breach of duty, neglect, error, misstatement, misleading statement, omissions, or act committed solely in the course of the activities of the Organization, including but not limited to...

*— National Union 49363 (12/89)*

It is common to see a provision excluding coverage for wrongful acts committed in the service of an entity other than the organization purchasing the coverage. You may not want to provide coverage for all of your board and staff members' volunteer activities. This harkens back to a fundamental tenet of risk management: do not assume liability for something or someone over which you do not have control. There are policies, however, that provide or can be endorsed to provide coverage for outside directorship liability with certain limitations.

7) **Coverage for Employment Practices**

Employment-related claims account for the vast majority of legal actions brought against nonprofits, nonprofit boards, and nonprofit managers and executives. And while there are many specific steps a nonprofit can and should take to reduce the likelihood of a claim, legal challenges cannot be avoided altogether without foregoing a workforce. Unless your agency has selected an alternative risk financing mechanism, liability insurance for employment-related actions is a wise investment. Today, most Commercial General Liability (CGL) policies contain an employment practices exclusion endorsement so coverage needs to be purchased elsewhere. A nonprofit has three ways to obtain such coverage. First, some companies offer an endorsement to the CGL policy. Second, your nonprofit can purchase a separate employment practices liability (EPL) policy. Third, many companies offer the coverage under a D&O policy, either by endorsement or as a part of the policy. Coverage under the D&O policy is the most common.

D&O policies provide employment practices coverage in one of two ways. Under the first form, the policy does not exclude employment-related claims specifically. The policy is "silent" on the matter and may be interpreted to provide coverage. However, there may be a breach of contract exclusion that will negate coverage. To rely on a policy that is silent on the topic of employment coverage, however, may be risky if employment practices liability is a significant exposure for your nonprofit and you do not have an alternative source of funding to pay for claims.

Under the second form of construction, the EPL coverage is described in some detail. Coverage, like other parts of a D&O policy, varies among companies. Some forms limit coverage to several causes of action, such as:

"Definition 2(h), "Wrongful Act" is amended in part to include the following:

6. Discrimination, whether based upon race, sex, age, national origin, religion, or disability; or

7. Sexual Harassment.

*— National Union 49363 (12/89)*

As indicated above, EPL coverage may be provided by an endorsement to a D&O policy. For example:

"It is agreed that Section 8.1, DEFINITIONS, shall be amended by adding the following:

Wrongful Act means any error, misstatement and misleading statement, act or omission, or neglect or breach of duty committed, attempted, or allegedly committed or attempted, by any Insured, individually or otherwise, in the discharge of his duties to the Association, or any matter claimed against him solely by reason of his serving in such capacity, including but not limited to, any actual or alleged wrongful dismissal, discharge or termination of employment, breach of any oral or written employment contract or quasi-employment contract, employment related misrepresentation, violation of employment discrimination laws (including workplace harassment), wrongful failure to employ or promote, wrongful discipline, wrongful deprivation of a career opportunity, failure to grant tenure, negligent evaluation, invasion of privacy, employment related defamation or employment related wrongful infliction of emotional distress. All such causally connected errors, statements, acts, omissions, neglects, breaches of duty or other such matters committed or attempted by, allegedly committed or attempted by, or claimed against one or more of the Insureds shall be deemed interrelated Wrongful Acts."

*— CHUBB, Form 14-02-1857 (Ed. 1/95)*

An alternative format for providing EPL coverage is to incorporate employment practices in the definition of wrongful act or claim or in a separate definition of "employment practices claim" such as:

"EMPLOYMENT PRACTICES CLAIM means any CLAIM brought by:

1. an applicant for employment with the ENTITY,

2. an employee of the ENTITY, or

3. former employee of the ENTITY,

wherein one or more of the following are alleged:

    a.   breach of actual or implied contract of employment.

    b.   violation of anti-discrimination statutes, including harassment,

    c.   libel or slander related to employment relationship with the ENTITY,

    d.   retaliation for exercise of public right or duty,

    e.   intentional or negligent infliction of emotional distress ARISING OUT OF employment relationship with the ENTITY, or

    f.   other claims for wrongful failure to hire or promote, wrongful demotion, or wrongful termination."

— *Coregis, COR.OOC.2043 (7/97)*

(D) **"Employment Practice Wrongful Act"** means any actual or alleged:

(1) wrongful termination of the employment of, or demotion of or failure or refusal to hire or promote, any person;

(2) Discrimination or sexual harassment adversely affecting any employee of, or applicant for employment with, the **Insured Entity**; or

(3) retaliatory treatment against an employee of the **Insured Entity** on account of such employee's exercise or attempted exercise of his or her rights under law.

— *Executive Risk Indemnity Inc., Form C22208 (9/96 ed.)*

## 8) **Defense Coverage**

A primary motivating factor for purchasing nonprofit D&O coverage is to have funds available to pay for a defense against allegations of improper conduct. Most nonprofits cannot fund the substantial costs of a legal defense. According to Watson Wyatt's Nonprofit Organization Directors & Officers Liability Survey Report (1993), the average cost to defend a lawsuit runs between $35,000 and $100,000. However, do not assume that your D&O insurer will defend the claim and pay defense costs as they are incurred.

Historically, under the corporate D&O policy it was the insured's duty to defend claims. An older Aetna policy states "(1) It shall be the duty of the **Insureds** and not the duty of Aetna to defend **Claims**. No **Defense Expenses** shall be incurred and no settlement of any **Claim** shall be made without Aetna's consent, such consent not to be unreasonably withheld." (F-1918 ED. 10-88) If the insurer does not have the duty to defend, the company may only reimburse the insured for these costs — the nonprofit must pay the expenses and then seek reimbursement from the insurance company. In many cases the insurer will not pay these expenses until the claim is resolved. However, some of these policies do provide for the advancement of defense costs or will pay expenses on a current basis (as the insured incurs them).

For example:

> (2)   Aetna shall, upon written request by an **Insured**, pay on a current basis **Defense Expenses** which are otherwise payable under this Policy, except to the extent that such **Defense Expenses** are being paid under the terms of any other policy or policies of insurance.
>
> — *Aetna, (F-1918) ED. 10-88*

Today, most nonprofit D&O policies state that the company will or shall have the right and duty to defend any claim (or suit), even if such claim is *groundless, false, or fraudulent.* Under the provisions of the insurer's duty to defend, the insurance company pays defense costs and expenses (up to the limit of liability), even when only a portion of the claim is covered under the policy.

Examples of "duty to defend" language include:

> "The Company shall have the right and duty to defend any Claim against the Member arising from a Wrongful Act, subject to the terms and provisions of this policy. Our right

and duty to defend end when we have used up the applicable limit of liability in the payment of Defense Costs, settlements and judgments. We may at our discretion investigate any allegation of a Wrongful Act and settle any Claim that may result. The Member shall give the Company such information and cooperation as it may reasonably require."

— *NIAC DO (7-98)*

"The Company shall have the right and duty to defend any Claim covered by this policy. Coverage shall apply even if any of the allegations are groundless, false or fraudulent. The Company's duty to defend shall cease upon exhaustion of the Company's applicable Limit of Liability set forth in Item 2 of the Declarations."

— *CHUBB, Form 14-02-2009 (Ed. 5/96)*

The policy may also include a provision that gives the nonprofit the opportunity to assume responsibility for the defense of the claim.

For example:

"The Insurer has the right and duty to defend all Claims, even if the allegations are groundless, false or fraudulent, or alternatively the Insurer may, at its option, give its written consent to the defense of any Claim by the Insureds. The Insurer's obligation to defend any Claim or pay any Loss, including Defense Costs, shall be completely fulfilled and extinguished if the Limit of Liability has been exhausted by payment of Loss."

— *CNA-G-20717-A (ED. 2/94)*

### 9) Selection of Defense Counsel

If your nonprofit is sued and the claim is covered by your D&O policy, do you expect to have a say in the selection of defense counsel? There is great variation in policy provisions and insurer practice with regard to the selection of defense counsel. Some insurers indicate that they prefer to retain control over the defense — control warranted by their substantial expertise in defending claims.

They know, for example, the best employment lawyers in a particular state. Other insurers see the insured as a full partner in the defense and prefer to receive the insured's input early on.

Large nonprofits are more likely to have ongoing relationships with counsel and may work with certain legal specialists, such as child welfare or employment law experts, on an ongoing basis. These nonprofits can argue that the use of a qualified attorney who already knows the organization could keep defense costs to a minimum. Other insurers contend that upon receiving notice of a claim, they seek to identify the best qualified counsel for that particular claim. The first correspondence the insured receives from the carrier may be a letter naming the attorney the insurer has retained to defend the nonprofit. Reference to the selection of defense counsel may or may not be included in a D&O policy. Many small nonprofits consider the insurer's role in appointing qualified defense counsel to be an important benefit of D&O coverage.

Where the insurer has an affirmative *duty to defend* that duty normally affords the insurer the right and discretion to appoint defense counsel. It is not always true, however, that under a policy where the insured must defend itself that it has the absolute right to select counsel. The insurer may retain some control over the selection of defense counsel even when the insured assumes responsibility for the defense. The insurer may insist on approving or consenting to the selection of counsel.

Examples of policy provisions on the selection of defense counsel include:

> "The Insured shall have the option to: (1) select his defense attorney or to consent to the Insurer's choice of defense attorney, which consent shall not be unreasonably withheld; and (2) participate in, and assist in the direction of, the defense of any claim."
>
> — *National Union 49363 (12/89)*

"As respects such insurance as is afforded by this policy, the Company shall:

A.   Have the right and duty to defend, including the selection of counsel, any CLAIM against the INSUREDS seeking damages for LOSS..."

— *Coregis, CFM 93.1.0494 (8/93)*

"It shall be the duty of the Insureds and not the duty of the Company to defend Claims made against the Insureds..."

— *The USLI Companies (215) 688-2535 DO-100 (1/94)*

(1)   It shall be the duty of the **Insureds** and not the duty of Aetna to defend **Claims**. No **Defense Expenses** shall be incurred and no settlement of any **Claim** shall be made without Aetna's consent, such consent not to be unreasonably withheld.

— *Aetna (F-1918) ED. 10-88*

## 10) **Defense Costs Outside the Policy Limits**

An increasingly common option in the nonprofit D&O marketplace is the availability of policies that provide coverage for defense costs outside or in addition to the limit of liability. For example, a nonprofit with a $1 million D&O limit is sued by a donor who alleges misuse of restricted grant funds. By the time the case is ready to go to trial, $120,000 in attorneys' fees have been incurred. The donor appears willing to settle the claim, but seeks the full amount of its original grant, $1 million. Under a "defense outside the limits" policy, the insured — the nonprofit — still has $1 million in coverage that can be used for settlement costs or a judicial verdict. Under a traditional policy, defense costs are included within the purchased limit of liability. In this case, only $880,000 would be remaining for settlement or to pay a judgment.

The wording in a "defense outside the limits" policy might look like:

"In addition to the applicable limit of liability, the Company shall pay:

All CLAIMS EXPENSES incurred in any action or suit brought against the INSURED alleging a WRONGFUL ACT,..."

— *Coregis, CFM 93.1.0494 (8/93)*

"Defense costs are in addition to the applicable Limit of Liability set forth in Item 3 of the Declarations, and the payment by the Company of Defense costs does not reduce such applicable Limit of Liability."

— *CHUBB, Form 14-022061 (Ed. 7/96)*

The option described above may be appealing to nonprofit managers who are fearful that defense costs will substantially diminish the amount available for a judgment or settlement. However, the additional coverage does not come without a price. Previously, with a policy that had defense costs within the limit of liability, the insurance company knew its maximum loss — the policy limit. Now, the insurance companies know that they will pay potentially substantial defense costs in addition to the policy limit. Therefore, the insurers usually charge a higher premium for the policies with defense costs outside of the limit. When comparing policies and pricing, make sure you determine whether defense costs are inside or outside the limits of each policy.

## 11) **Reasonable Deductible**

A number of years ago, it was virtually impossible to purchase a nonprofit D&O policy that did not feature a deductible or retention. Since some policies still contain a deductible or retention, it is worth knowing the difference between the two. Through the years, the insurance industry has blurred the distinction between retentions and deductibles. Therefore, the following explanation is not universal, like so many other aspects of insurance; it depends upon how your policy defines the term. The term used in your D&O policy may or may not be consistent with the classic definitions noted below. Read the policy carefully to determine what applies in your particular case.

A deductible is the amount of the loss that the insured must pay. If you have a $500 deductible, the insurance company will calculate the final loss costs and subtract the amount of the deductible to determine their payment. Some companies will pay the full amount of the loss and then seek repayment from the insured for the amount of the deductible. Other companies will calculate the final loss payment, subtract the amount of the deductible, and issue a check for the reduced amount. The insured must then pay the balance to the claimant.

A retention is a little more stringent in that the insurance company will not pay anything until the insured has paid expenses equal to the retention. If you have a $2,500 retention, your nonprofit will pay the first $2,500 in defense or settlement expenses — the insurance company may send you the bills equal to your retention. After you pay the retention, the insurer will pay the other expenses up to the policy limit and subject to the policy terms. Under some nonprofit D&O policies the retention does not apply to defense costs. Under this type of policy, if a claim incurs no settlement costs and only incurs legal fees, the nonprofit does not have to pay the retention. Some older D&O policies require the insured to pay both a large retention and a percentage of each loss. If the loss after the retention was $100,000 and the policy had a 10 percent retention, the insured would pay $10,000 and the company $90,000. Today, policies with percentage retentions are very rare.

Most D&O policies prohibit the insured from insuring the amount of the deductible or retention. This practice originated when insurance companies first started writing D&O coverage. They wrote the first policies with very large retentions or deductibles of $25,000 or more. The insurers wanted the insured to have a financial stake and incentive to avoid activities that could generate a claim.

Another nuance with deductibles is how they are applied. Some forms include an "each Insured Person each Claim" deductible that applies to each director or officer named in each claim. With this format, the deductible amount would add up quickly. However, often the company then caps the deductible total by setting an "all Insured

Persons" deductible. This is similar to an "aggregate" limit on the deductible.

Occasionally, a company will offer an "aggregate" deductible. On the "per claim" basis, the insured pays the deductible each and every time a claim is made under the policy. This expense can be considerable if multiple claims are filed against a nonprofit in a single year. In the latter example, the insured pays the "per claim" deductibles until the payments equal the aggregate amount. Then the deductible no longer applies for that policy year.

As the insurance marketplace for nonprofit D&O insurance became more competitive, the requirements for deductibles and retentions lowered. Today, many insurers write D&O policies with a "zero" deductible or retention.

The purpose of a deductible is twofold. First, the deductible will cover the smaller losses that the insured can afford to pay. Secondly, a deductible encourages the insured to avoid or prevent losses. However, competition has minimized the insurance companies' demand for deductibles. The lack of a deductible or retention is very appealing to most nonprofits.

A deductible is one form of the risk financing technique called retention because the nonprofit has to pay that amount of the loss. As with all retention options, the organization should decide how much it can afford to retain and the costs-benefits of a higher retention. In the past, nonprofits had very little choice in the amount of the D&O deductible or retention — $2,500 was often the minimum. Today, the nonprofit buyer has choices. The first decision is whether or not you want to retain some part of the loss, and if so how much. One of the factors to consider is how much the premium will be reduced if the nonprofit elects a large deductible or retention. You should evaluate the costs and benefits of the higher retention. For larger organizations the premium savings may be sizable and the higher retention justified. For smaller nonprofits, a relatively small premium savings is simply not worth the burden of a higher deductible. Another factor to consider is whether you are purchasing the D&O insurance to protect the organization from a catastrophic loss or to pay for all losses. Also, review what your policy covers, if it does not cover the expenses associated with administrative or regulatory proceedings, you are already retaining a significant exposure.

## 12) Coverage for Professional Services

As you have no doubt realized by this point, D&O policies differ. One distinction is in the type of policies offered by insurers. Several years ago, companies introduced an association/organization professional liability policy that incorporates D&O coverage with other coverages. It is very popular with nonprofit associations as well as professional service organizations, such as nonprofit law firms. Under an organization/association professional liability policy, coverage may include the coverages associated with personal injury (libel, slander, malicious prosecution, false arrest, etc.) and publishers liability (infringement of copyright or trademark, plagiarism, misappropriation of ideas). Usually the policy will refer to "Personal Injury and Publishers Liability" coverage or define "Personal Injury Wrongful Act." The definition of Wrongful Act will be such as:

> (Q) **"Wrongful Act"** means:
>
> (1) any **Employment Practices Wrongful Act** or **Personal Injury Wrongful Act** or other actual or alleged act, error, omission, misstatement, misleading statement or breach of duty by an **Insured Person** in his or her capacity as such;
>
> — *Executive Risk Indemnity Inc., Form C22208 (9/96 ed.)*

A number of D&O policies also provide coverage for professional services. The coverage is generally provided in one of three ways. First, the policy does not exclude professional services specifically therefore it can be argued that it is included. The second method is when the policy enumerates professional services or liability as covered. Lastly, a few professional liability policies may provide D&O coverage as an adjunct.

It is important to remember that a D&O policy does not provide coverage for bodily injury or property damage claims. Therefore, a D&O policy that provides coverage for professional services is not a substitute for a professional liability policy. Many nonprofits may provide services of a professional nature, such as health screening or service delivery, cosmetic services (beauticians, barbers), home health care, legal services, counseling, and physical therapy. For these organizations, the professional services coverage provided by the D&O policy is inappropriate for their needs. Remember, the D&O policy covers "wrongful acts" not negligent actions that result in bodily injury or property damage.

## D. Policy Nuances

Due to the diversity of D&O policies, it is critical for you to read the entire policy to understand the coverages provided. Insurance policies often appear to provide coverage to only then remove the coverage through an exclusion or limiting provision. In this section, we discuss some of the more subtle provisions of nonprofit D&O policies.

### ■ The Hammer Clause

A hammer clause is a policy provision that acts as a financial incentive for an insured to agree to a settlement proposed by the insurer. Under a traditional hammer clause, if an insured refuses to consent to a settlement proposed by the insurer and acceptable to the plaintiff, the insured will be responsible for negotiating and defending the claim at their own expense. The company's payment will not exceed the amount for which the claim could have been settled including defense costs up to that point. If the eventual loss is greater than the proposed settlement amount, the insured must pay the difference plus any defense costs incurred after the date on which the settlement was proposed. Hammer clauses serve a very specific purpose: they protect insurance companies from idealistic insureds bent on "fighting to the death" or "taking this case to the Supreme Court." While few, if any, insurers will remove the hammer clause, it is essential that you understand what the clause means. When you purchase $1 million in D&O liability coverage, you are not buying the right to spend up to the policy limit on a particular claim.

A typical hammer clause reads as follows:

"...the insurer may make any settlement of any claim it deems expedient with respect to any insured subject to such insured's written consent. If any insured withholds consent to such settlement, the insurer's liability for all loss on account of such claim shall not exceed the amount for which the insurer could have settled such claim plus defense costs incurred as of the date such settlement was proposed in writing by the insurer."

### ■ Insured vs. Insured Exclusion

This exclusion negates coverage for claims arising from one insured (person or entity) alleging misconduct by another insured. This exclusion may be significant if the policy includes any "Additional Insureds" by eliminating coverage for a claim made by an additional insured. If the policy includes coverage for wrongful employment acts, it will exempt employment claims from this exclusion. Otherwise, the insured vs. insured exclusion would automatically eliminate coverage for an EPL claim. For example:

5.   EXCLUSIONS

"This policy does not apply to any:

L.   Claim or Claims brought or maintained by any past or present Member, or any affiliate of the Organization. However, this exclusion shall not apply to: (1) Claims brought on behalf of the Organization by an Attorney General, or (2) Claims attributable to or arising out of employment practices, but only as those practices pertain to employees."

— NIAC DO (7/98)

Another form of an insured vs. insured exclusion serves to exclude certain types of claims.

For example:

> "The Insurer shall not be liable to pay any Loss in connection with any Claim: by the Entity or derivatively on behalf of the Entity by any directors or trustees of the Entity, or by any Affiliates or derivatively on behalf of any affiliate."
>
> — *CNA G-20717-A (Ed. 2/94)*

## ■ Contractual Liability or Breach of Contract Exclusion

Another common exclusion in a D&O policy excludes coverage for liability under any contract or agreement. If EPL coverage is provided, this provision should include a statement indicating that it does not apply to employment contracts. The idea behind this exclusion is that covering contract disputes would create a disincentive for a nonprofit to contract and fulfill its business obligations responsibly. Examples of contractual exclusions:

> (1) Solely with respect to Claims against the Insured Entity:
>
> (a) except for Claims for Employment Practices Wrongful Acts, Aetna shall not pay Loss, including Defense Expenses, for Claims for any actual or alleged liability under any contract or agreement, except for liability which would have attached even in the absence of such contract or agreement;
>
> — *Aetna, Endorsement N-302.7 (4-94) rev.*

> J. Any claims, demands or actions seeking relief or redress for either a willful, intentional, knowing, tortious or negligent breach of, failure to perform in whole or part, any oral, written or implied contract between the **INSUREDS** and any other person, except oral, written or implied contract relating to that person's employment by the **INSUREDS**.
>
> — *Coregis, CFM 93.1.0494 (8/93)*

## ■ Coverage for Subsidiaries

Policies may specifically include or exclude coverage for nonprofit subsidiaries of the Named Insured, including those created after the inception of the policy.

■ **ERISA Liability**

Most policies contain an exclusion covering claims based on the nonprofit's actual or alleged violation of its responsibilities as fiduciaries by the Employee Retirement Income Security Act of 1974 and any subsequent amendments or similar laws. The primary reason for this exclusion is that coverage for this fiduciary liability is available under a different policy. Some companies extend this exclusion to apply to the mismanagement of any employee benefit plan (health insurance, disability plans, life insurance, etc.). Recently, however, a number of insurers have announced plans to omit or modify this exclusion in their D&O policies.

■ **Innocent Insured Provision**

As indicated previously, D&O policies do not provide coverage for illegal acts. Coverage may be afforded, however, up until the time that criminal conduct has been proven in a court of law. In many cases, one insured may be guilty of a criminal act while all insured persons under the policy are named as defendants in a suit. In other cases, one or more insureds (but not all) under the policy may have committed a willful violation of civil law. The "innocent insured" provision reinstates coverage for any insured person that did not know about or participate in any form of wrongdoing — criminal or civil — specifically excluded under the policy.

# Chapter 5
# Reading Your Insurance Policy

*A*n insurance policy is a contract that defines the obligations of both the insured and the insurer. Most insurance policies contain terms that are hard to understand and written in a confusing manner. Taking the time to understand your policies is well worth the effort. Besides providing coverage, policies also assign certain responsibilities to the insured. Your failure to meet these obligations may impair the coverage.

Every insurance policy contains four key components: *declarations, insuring agreements, exclusions, and conditions.* Most policies also contain *endorsements.* The *Definitions* section is also an important part of every policy. Knowledge of these components will help you understand what your policy does and does not cover, and what your responsibilities are when filing a claim. It is important to read and make certain you understand the policy definitions before proceeding to other key sections.

***Declarations*** is the first page of the policy that summarizes key information. The "dec page" shows the insured's name and address, the policy period, amount of deductibles (if any), the pending or prior acts date (or retroactive date), and other information specific to that policy.

***Insuring Agreements*** specify what the insurance company has agreed to pay for or to provide in exchange for the premium. These are usually found in the first section of the policy and are clearly identified. However, there may be other insuring agreements buried in the policy and are often called coverages. An insurance policy starts by declaring what it covers and then proceeds to restrict, limit, and exclude certain coverages. Therefore, you cannot just read the Insuring Agreement to understand the coverage. For example, under a D&O policy, the insuring agreement says that "the company will pay on behalf of the insured all loss that the insured becomes legally obligated to pay due to a claim first made against the insured during the policy period because of a wrongful act." As you read the policy, you must research the definitions of insured, loss, claim, policy period, and wrongful act in order to determine if the policy will cover the incident and for whom.

**Exclusions** are the policy provisions that eliminate coverage for specified exposures or actions. Exclusions clarify the coverages granted by the policy. Most policies have a section entitled, "Exclusions," however, exclusionary language appears in other parts of the policy. Also, sometimes an exclusion contains a broadening provision such as a contractual exclusion that does not apply to an employment practices claim.

**Conditions** qualify the promises made by the insurance company. The company imposes certain requirements or conditions on the insured, such as providing written notice of claim as soon as practicable to a specified address. Review the policy carefully to identify all of the conditions that you must follow. Failure to meet your obligations can void the policy or otherwise restrict coverage.

**Endorsements** are policy forms that modify the main coverage form. Endorsements can add coverage (adding Employment Practices Liability) or they can modify the coverage by revising a definition (providing coverage for nonmonetary claims). Lastly, an endorsement can restrict or exclude coverage such as an endorsement that excludes claims from pending and prior litigation.

***Definitions*** explain the special meaning within an insurance context of many common words. Most insurance companies identify these special words by bold print, all capital letters or quotation marks. Read the definitions section closely since it often restricts or limits coverage.

An insurance contract is a complex contract with conflicting and confusing provisions. You must read the *entire* contract to understand fully the coverages, the insurance company's responsibilities, and your obligations. Some insurance advisors recommend that buyers review the endorsements first to identify those sections of the main policy form altered by the endorsements. This makes the process of reading the main form easier by alerting the reader in advance to sections deleted or altered via endorsement.

As legal documents, the courts have scrutinized many insurance policies. Unfortunately, the various courts have rendered conflicting interpretations. In contrast, most losses do not involve complex policy interpretations — the insurance company and insured quickly agree that the policy covers the loss. However, you must know your duties and responsibilities in order to qualify for coverage. Take the time to understand your D&O policy. Your insurance advisor can help you with this task.

It's a fact of life today that businesses and nonprofits alike need to take precautions to protect themselves. Being ready to face any potential risk means you'll avoid being caught off guard. Selecting the right insurance is one of the best ways to be prepared. Although choosing a D&O insurance policy can seem like a daunting task, with a little preparation and research, your efforts will guide your organization through most any hardship that comes along.

# Appendix A:
# D&O Buying Tips

■ Solicit competitive bids on your insurance program every three-to-five years. Competition is one way to determine whether you're paying a fair price. However, be careful that the policies offer comparable coverage — a lower premium often means less coverage or the insurer may be "low-balling" to sign you up. Future increases may be necessary.

■ Allow sufficient time for an underwriting review — particularly with a carrier unfamiliar with your nonprofit.

■ Fully complete the carrier's application and attach all requested supporting information. The information requested generally includes your bylaws, board roster, and audited financial statements or IRS Form 990. Some carriers request a copy of your employee handbook. Present your nonprofit in the best light and emphasize any activities underway to minimize losses, such as training supervisors on employment practices. Do not view the application process as a burdensome paperwork requirement, but as an opportunity to protect your nonprofit and conserve scarce resources.

■ Identify an insurance advisor — a broker, agent, or consultant — with experience working with nonprofits. A specialist can be invaluable as you try to understand the D&O options available to your nonprofit.

- Be accurate and truthful in answering questions on the application. Misstatements on the application may void coverage if discovered upon the filing of a claim.

- Respond to the underwriter's questions (usually conveyed through your insurance advisor) promptly.

- Fully disclose your nonprofit's prior losses and provide details on corrective action taken to avoid future losses.

- Remember that coverage and pricing terms are negotiable. If any specific terms are unacceptable, propose alternatives. For example, if coverage for employment practices is excluded, inquire about purchasing coverage via endorsement. Or, if the policy indicates that the insurer has sole authority to appoint defense counsel, inquire about the possibility of a policy form that allows the insured to participate in the selection of counsel.

- Review the extent of the "prior acts" coverage provided by the policy. Seek coverage for incidents dating back to the inception of the nonprofit. (A great deal if you can get it!) If the policy contains a retroactive date make sure that the date stays the same with each renewal or new policy.

- Make certain that any prior incidents that might potentially give rise to a claim are reported on your application to a new carrier as well as to your existing carrier. Claims stemming from known incidents will be excluded under your new policy.

- Request information on the carrier's financial strength and status ("admitted" versus "surplus lines") and have your broker explain the ratings to you. Ask your broker about the carrier's history on handling D&O claims against nonprofits. If you're considering an alternative market (i.e. a charitable risk pool, or risk retention group), or a sponsored insurance program, make similar inquiries.

- Consider the benefit of various loss control programs offered by your D&O carrier. With an estimated 60 companies now offering nonprofit D&O coverage, a growing number are providing useful loss prevention services, such as access to toll free employment practices hot lines. Risk education services can greatly enhance a D&O insurance program. Ask about available services when you request a quotation.

# Appendix B:
# Frequently Asked Questions About D&O

❑ *We think we need D&O but we can't afford it.*
*What should we do?*

Many nonprofits, particularly those that are newly formed or in the start-up mode, report some difficulty affording the cost of D&O insurance. Nonprofit buyers have many options. Those wishing to shave dollars off the annual premium can often do so by choosing only those policy provisions considered most critical. Many insurers offer a range of policy forms containing various provisions. For example, a volunteer-run nonprofit without paid staff may forego employment practices coverage until it hires staff. Two other alternatives are available. First, some insurance agencies offer premium financing — even on a relatively low cost liability policy. If affording a lump sum premium is a concern, inquire about the availability of premium financing from your insurance provider. Finally, some start-up nonprofits address the question of cost by charging each board member a fraction of the policy premium.

❑ *How do we know if we're paying too much for*
*D&O?*

As you have read, there is great variation among nonprofit D&O policies. Due to the differences in coverages, premiums will vary, too. When evaluating D&O policy costs, you have to review the premium in relation to the policy's coverages, limits and deductibles. Another way to determine if you are paying too much is to request quotations from different insurance companies. As mentioned earlier, we recommend securing competitive bids every three to five years.

❑ *Several members of our board are active on other nonprofit boards. Will our D&O policy protect their outside activities?*

Most policies exclude coverage for claims resulting from any insured serving another organization. The rationale is that as a long-standing rule of risk management, "don't assume liability for activities that you don't control." Check your policy for a provision that limits or excludes coverage for "outside" board or volunteer activities.

❑ *We just learned about the Volunteer Protection Act. Does it mean we can cancel our D&O coverage?*

The Volunteer Protection Act (VPA) provides that, if a volunteer meets certain criteria, he or she has a defense to a suit alleging simple or "mere" negligence and cannot be held responsible ("liable") for that alleged wrongdoing. In cases where the volunteer does not meet the Act's criteria, he may still enjoy some measure of protection as long as he has not engaged in conduct that is specifically prohibited. The VPA preempts the laws of any state, except in cases where a state provides greater protection from liability, or in cases where the state has eliminated applicability due to the fact that all parties to an action are citizens of a state.

While the VPA may achieve its principal goal of reducing the disparity in the existing state liability laws, unfortunately it has led to the circulation of many misrepresentations of its intent and effect. The law is also sufficiently vague so as to make it difficult to predict how it will be interpreted by the courts. It will be some time before we can thoughtfully analyze judicial interpretations of the Act. In the meantime, many volunteers will continue to view the VPA as providing complete protection against lawsuits. And many nonprofit managers and board members will put their organizations in jeopardy of financial ruin by assuming the promise of "protection" suggested by the legislation.

It is critically important to remember what the VPA doesn't do:

1. **The VPA does not prohibit lawsuits against volunteers.** Volunteers may be sued for their actions or inactions. If sued personally — and without the promise of indemnification from the sponsor nonprofit — a volunteer will still be required to mount a legal defense. This typically involves hiring counsel, appearing in court, and paying necessary fees.

2. **The VPA does not shield a volunteer from the frustration, time, or expense associated with defending a lawsuit.** The fact that judgments against volunteers are extremely rare is of little solace to those that have been sued. It is unlikely that the VPA will result in the quick dismissal of lawsuits against volunteers, thereby avoiding the frustration and time involved in mounting a defense.

3. **The VPA does not prohibit lawsuits against nonprofits** or limit the liability of an organization for harm caused by volunteers. In fact, the sponsor of the original bill — Congressman John Porter — intended the opposite. Porter stated that "The idea here is that if litigation must arise from volunteer activity, the nonprofit organization itself should be named, not individual volunteers."

4. **The VPA does not provide any protection for the most common sources of lawsuits against volunteers.** Claims alleging the negligent operation of a motor vehicle, and employment-related claims alleging violation of federal or state civil rights laws are specifically excluded from coverage under the VPA.

5. **The VPA does not negate the need for liability insurance.** While a variety of tools are available for financing risk, many nonprofits choose insurance as the preferred financing strategy. Judgments against nonprofits are relatively rare. However, substantial defense costs are likely any time a lawsuit is filed. Since the VPA does not stop

someone from filing suit, exposure to costly legal fees is always possible. Liability coverage that pays the cost of a legal defense may protect a nonprofit from ruin.

❑ ***Doesn't my homeowner's policy provide coverage for directors and officers?***

Most homeowner's policies do not cover the D&O peril of "wrongful acts." The homeowner's policy covers the legal obligations to pay damages because of bodily injury or property damage, although some policies also include personal injury (libel, slander, defamation, invasion of privacy, etc.). Consequently, a homeowner's policy will only pay for your negligent acts that result in bodily injury or damage to the property of others — it will not respond if you are accused of violating someone's civil rights (employment practices) or mismanaging the organization.

A few insurance companies do extend coverage for board activities through their "prestige" or "high-end" homeowner's policies. Check with your personal insurance advisor to determine if your policy provides or can be endorsed to cover your board activities.

❑ ***Directors and officers are insureds under my commercial general liability policy. Why do I need D&O?***

Including volunteers under a commercial general liability policy (CGL) is a good idea but it does not provide "complete" protection. A CGL policy insures a nonprofit for very different types of claims than a Directors' & Officers' Liability policy. The general liability policy protects the organization, its directors, officers, employees and volunteers (if endorsed as an Additional Insured) for claims arising from bodily injury and property damage. The policy covers the negligent acts of the "insureds" that cause injury to another person or damage to the property of another (subject to policy provisions).

In contrast, a D&O policy insures against the "wrongful acts" of the organization, its directors, officers, employees and volunteers (depending upon the definition of

"Insured"). Each policy defines "wrongful act" differently, but in general it means the actual or alleged acts or omissions including breaches of duty that the directors, officers or other insureds may perform. Most D&O policies exclude coverage for bodily injury or property damage, unless the policy includes Employment Practices Liability (EPL) coverage. The EPL form usually includes coverage for emotional distress and other bodily injury type allegations contained within the claim.

Since these two policies cover very different risks, the D&O policy should also include volunteers as "insureds." Most nonprofits use committees to perform many of the governance and management functions. The membership of the various committees often includes non-board member volunteers. For example, a Risk Management Committee can include board members, an insurance agent, an attorney and other volunteers. The committee and its members could be named in a claim alleging that the committee failed to purchase adequate insurance. A commercial general liability policy would not cover this claim since the occurrence does not include bodily injury or property damage. A D&O policy would probably respond (subject to policy provisions) to the allegation of a "wrongful act." Therefore, each organization should evaluate its own insurance needs and consider purchasing both D&O and commercial general liability insurance policies.

❑ *Our state law protects us from suits against our directors and officers — isn't that enough?*

In all but a handful of states — New Jersey and Virginia are examples — the doctrine of charitable immunity has been abolished. In states that do not recognize charitable immunity, nonprofits can and are held responsible for negligence stemming from foreseeable harm. During the past decade, nearly every state has adopted volunteer protection legislation. These laws provided limited immunity for certain volunteers — not nonprofits — under certain circumstances. The federal Volunteer Protection Act preempts state laws except when they specifically provide greater protection. The VPA and its state-based counterparts do not prohibit suits. Even if one of these laws allows your volunteers to escape liability, substantial funds are required to defend even a frivolous claim. D&O coverage typically covers the defense costs as they are incurred.

### ❏ *Is an employee handbook a good idea?*

Employment attorneys disagree on the value of an employee handbook or personnel policies manual. Some argue that it provides an appropriate statement of various employment policies and helps ensure wide understanding of the policies. Others argue that it may convert the at-will employment relationship to a contractual one, therein imposing additional duties on the nonprofit. Employment law experts agree on one thing — a nonprofit employer that ignores its handbook is at greater risk than an organization that operates without a handbook. A nonprofit should never develop and adopt any policy or handbook, employment or otherwise, that it is unwilling or unable to follow. Many nonprofits get into trouble when they fail to keep their handbooks up-to-date, do not insist that all staff be familiar with the provisions in the handbook, or randomly exempt certain employees from the directives in the handbook. Whether or not a nonprofit uses an employment handbook, the following risk management practices are important:

- Ensure that the organization's personnel policies are clear, consistent and within the law;

- Make certain that the nonprofit conveys its employment policies to its employees in a clear and concise manner;

- Ensure that the organization fulfills its end of the employment relationship; and

- Seek legal counsel before taking any adverse employment action.

❑ **Is there any wisdom in including related entities that are separately incorporated with separate boards?**

That depends. The problem with including additional entities under one D&O policy is the dissolution of the policy limit. The policy limit under some D&O policies is the "maximum aggregate limit of liability for all Claims made or deemed made during the year." Therefore, each time a claim is made, the defense costs and settlement are subtracted from the policy limit and once that sum is used the organization no longer has any coverage. Other D&O policies provide an "each loss" limit, and also include an "each policy year" limit that is usually the same amount.

If you are going to include additional entities under your D&O policy, we strongly recommend that you increase the policy limit to compensate for the additional exposures. A $1 million limit does not mean that each entity has a full $1 million of coverage. However, if all that the entities can afford is one D&O policy with a low limit, that option is arguably better than no coverage at all.

❑ **We have only two employees so there is no real need for D&O if it covers employment practices for the most part. What other claims are likely?**

As indicated under Chapter 1, in addition to employees, sources of claims against nonprofits include funders, regulatory agencies, service recipients, and third parties. A funder may allege the misuse of or failure to account for grant money, a third party may allege breach of contract and related claims, and a service recipient may allege negligent hiring and supervision by the nonprofit's management and board of directors. Finally, even nonprofits with as few as one employee may face employment-related claims. In a recent case in California a nonprofit's sole employee was fired by the board and alleged wrongful termination and age discrimination. Although the nonprofit was granted a motion for summary judgement, more than $75,000 in defense costs were incurred.

# Glossary of Terms

*T*his glossary is designed to be a reference for nonprofit managers and volunteers. The definitions are applicable to the nonprofit sector. Although accurate, the definitions vary from those the reader might find in a law dictionary or insurance text.

**Avoidance** — Risk management strategy in which a nonprofit avoids an activity or service that it considers too risky.

**Board of directors** — Governance body of a nonprofit made up of individuals who are appointed or elected and whose function it is to provide policy, and sometimes management, direction for the purpose of accomplishing the organization's mission.

**Bylaws** — Set of rules that outline how a nonprofit organization operates, including rules describing key positions and their respective duties, election of officers, frequency of board meetings, and quorum requirements.

**Care, Duty of** — Standard of behavior required by a nonprofit board member or officer in making decisions. The standard is to use the level of care that a reasonably prudent person would exercise in a similar situation.

**Charitable immunity** — Legal defense, now largely defunct, by which charitable organizations were protected from litigation by virtue of their charitable status.

**Commercial General Liability (CGL) insurance** — Insurance that covers claims filed by another party (i.e. clients, general public) alleging bodily injury, personal injury and/or property damage arising from the nonprofit's business premises or operations.

**Deductible** — Amount deducted from a loss. The deductible is an amount assumed in advance by an insured as a means of obtaining a lower premium for the coverage.

**Defendant** — Individual or organization against whom a lawsuit has been brought.

**Directors' & Officers' (D&O) Liability Insurance** — Insurance that provides coverage against "wrongful acts" which might include actual or alleged errors, omissions, misleading statements, and neglect or breach of duty on the part of the board of directors.

**Employee** — Individual who is paid to perform specific duties under the direction and control of the organization. The individual is provided with a wage or salary, and sometimes benefits. The individual's status is specified as an employee, as opposed to an independent contractor, as determined by the IRS 20 Point Test.

**Employment Practices Liability Insurance (EPLI)** — Insurance that provides coverage for claims arising out of employment practices. EPLI policies generally cover the organization, its directors, officers, and employees.

**Endorsement** — Document specifying changes to the coverage afforded by a specific insurance policy.

**Exclusion** — Provision within an insurance policy that specifies the perils or conditions that are not covered.

**Immunity** — A provision in the law which shields a person or organization from legal obligations.

**Indemnify** — Compensate for actual losses sustained.

**Insurance** — A contract whereby an organization agrees to indemnify another and to pay a specified amount upon determinable contingencies in exchange for a premium.

**Joint liability** — A form of liability in which the liability is shared by more than one person.

**Joint and several liability** — A form of liability in which all of the individuals involved are fully liable as individuals and also as members of a group.

**Liability** — Any enforceable legal obligation.

**Loyalty, Duty of** — Standard of behavior that requires a director or officer (of a board) to pursue the interests of the organization, particularly financial, rather than his/her own or the interests of another person. To place the organization's interests ahead of his/her own.

**Minutes** — Minutes are a summary and documentation of a board meeting. The specifications for acceptable minutes will vary with the organization, but should include who attended the meeting, the significant issues discussed, the actions taken on motions and resolutions, and reports of officers or committees.

**Modification** — Modification is a risk management technique that involves changing the activity so that the chance of harm occurring and impact of potential damage are within acceptable limits.

**Negligence** — Failure to use the standard of care that a reasonably prudent person would exercise in a similar circumstance.

**Nonprofit Corporation Act** — State legislation that provides for the establishment and operation of nonprofit corporations. The legislation outlines the rights and duties of nonprofit corporations in addition to specifying rules for the election of officers, holding of meetings and procedures for the dissolution, liquidation or other changes in the organization's legal status.

**Nonprofit (or not-for-profit) organization** — An organization in which no part of its income is distributable to its members, directors, officers, stockholders or other individuals and that meets the state statute designation of a nonprofit entity. *Note:* While most people equate nonprofit organizations with charitable or 501(c)(3) entities (those that are eligible to receive tax deductible contributions), other categories of nonprofits exist as well, including trade associations and labor unions. An organization need not be tax-exempt to be recognized and organized as a "nonprofit" under state law.

**Nonprofit sector** (also called independent sector, charitable sector, voluntary sector or tax-exempt sector) — A collection of organizations that are formally constituted, private (as opposed to governmental), serve some public purpose, self-governing, voluntary, and non-profit-distributing.

**Obedience, Duty of** — Standard of care that obligates a director or officer (of a board) to act in a manner that demonstrates faithfulness to the organization's mission and obeys all applicable laws, statutes and regulations.

**Officer** — Individual who has a fiduciary responsibility within a nonprofit. This individual can be a member of the organization's board, executive committee, or an employee of the organization.

**Personal injury liability** — Injury to a person or organization that arises out of incidences of libel, slander, invasion of privacy, false arrest or detention, malicious prosecution, or wrongful entry or eviction.

**Personally liable** — Liability that an individual assumes when he/she is directly involved in the occurrence and cannot defer the liability to another person or entity.

**Plaintiff** — Individual or organization that initiates a lawsuit to obtain a remedy for an injury.

**Punitive damages** — Damages awarded by the court to an individual in excess of those required to compensate the plaintiff for the loss sustained. These damages are a type of punishment for the offender for failing to take proper care and usually involves wanton or willful misconduct.

**Quorum** — The minimum number of individuals required in the bylaws to be present to conduct business at a meeting.

**D&O: What You Need to Know**

**Respondeat superior** — Legal principle by which employers are held responsible for the actions of those they supervise. Literally, the "master" shall answer for the acts of his "servant." In the context of volunteer organizations, the nonprofit is the "master" and the volunteers and employees are the "servants" working on the organization's behalf.

**Retention** — A tool or technique in risk management whereby the nonprofit accepts all or a portion of the risk and prepares for the consequences. A deductible on an insurance policy is a form of retention.

**Risk** — Any threat or possibility of loss that will endanger an organization's ability to accomplish its mission.

**Risk evaluation and prioritization** — A step in the risk management process that examines the possibility of each risk becoming reality and estimates its probable effect and cost to the nonprofit. Organizations should examine their records to determine the frequency and severity of common risks.

**Risk identification** — The first step in the risk management process that identifies the risks that are relevant to the organization.

**Risk management** — A discipline for dealing with uncertainty.

**Risk management techniques** — Strategies for controlling risk which include avoidance, modification, sharing and retention.

**Risk modification** — The means of changing an activity so that the chance of harm occurring and impact of potential damage are within acceptable limits.

**Risk sharing** — A risk management tool whereby an organization shares a risk with another organization. Traditionally, risk management literature has referred to this option as "transfer" because of the presumption that it is possible to transfer risk to another party. However, although insurance will pay for the financial consequences of a loss, it does not fund the potential loss of donors, volunteers and clients if the nonprofit's reputation is damaged. Examples of risk sharing include mutual aid agreements with other nonprofits, purchasing insurance, and sharing responsibility for a risk with another through a contractual agreement.

**Staff** — volunteers and employees who carry out the work of an organization.

**Ultra vires** — An act that is considered beyond the scope of authority (as defined in the organization's legal documents) of an organization, such as an action taken by the board of directors of a nonprofit organization.

**Vicarious liability** — Liability imposed on a person or organization for the acts, errors or omissions of persons serving on its behalf. Vicarious liability can be imposed even if the individual or organization is not directly involved in the occurrence. The liability of one party is imputed to another.

**Volunteer** — Individual who freely provides services to an organization without compensation other than reimbursement for reasonable expenses.

## Sources

Giftis, Steven H. *Law Dictionary*. Woodbury, N.Y.: Barron's Educational Series, Inc., 1975.

Hopkins, Bruce R. *Nonprofit Law Dictionary*. New York: John Wiley & Sons, Inc., 1994.

Lai, Mary L., Chapman, Terry S., Steinbock, Elmer L. *Am I Covered For...?* 2d ed., San Jose, CA: Human Services Inc., 1984.

Lorimer, James J., Perlet, Harry P., Kempkin, Rederick G., Hodosh, Frederick, H. *The Legal Environment of Insurance, Volumes I and II*. Malvern, PA: AICPCU

Salamon, Lester M., *America's Nonprofit Sector: A Primer*, The Foundation Center, 1992.